9 2014
MAR - 1 2014

MAKES
PERFECT®

Writing Chinese Characters

Zhe Jiaoshe with Fu Zheng, translator

Mc
Graw
Hill
Education

New York Chicago San Francisco Athens London Madrid
Mexico City Milan New Delhi Singapore Sydney Toronto

1 2 3 4 5 6 7 8 9 0   RHR/RHR   1 0 9 8 7 6 5 4 3

ISBN   978-0-07-182803-1
MHID   0-07-182803-6

Library of Congress Control Number: 2013934653

McGraw-Hill Education books are available at special quantity discounts to use as premiums and sales promotions or for use in corporate training programs. To contact a representative, please visit the Contact Us pages at www.mhprofessional.com.

This book is printed on acid-free paper.

Contents 目 录

An overview of Chinese calligraphy
中国书法艺术概况

The art of Chinese calligraphy evolved throughout Chinese history. Chinese calligrapher is a form of visual art based on dots and lines that expresses the distinct styles of the calligrapher. Written with brush pens, Chinese calligraphy is regarded as the pure and indigenous form of Chinese art. There are five schools of Chinese scripts which developed from different periods of time in history: the Seal Script(Zhuan Shu), the Official Script(Li Shu), the Running Script(Cao Shu), the Cursive Script(Xing Shu) and the Regular Script (Kai Shu). Each script carries distinct style and techniques.

The Seal Script is the earliest form of writing characterized by simple pen-craft and high decorative value. It can be classified into the Oracle style (sixteenth century BC), the Big-seal style(eleventh century BC) and the Small-seal style(211 BC). The most famous Seal Script calligrapher is Li Si.

The Official Script evolved from the Seal Script and is written in a faster pace. It flourished in the Han Dynasty and is also called "Han Li." It has a history of more than 2000 years.

The Running Script is a simplified form of the standardized Seal Script and Official Script. It developed into a relatively independent style during the Han Dynasty. The Running Script is divided into Zhang Cao, Big Running Script, and Small Running Script. Wang Xizhi, his son Wang Xianzhi in Jin Dynasty (265—420 AD) and Monk Zhiyong in Sui Dynasty（581—618 AD）were the best known calligraphers of this school.

The Cursive Script is a script that combines the characteristics of the Regular Script and the Running Script. Unlike the Seal Script and the Running Scripts, which are less legible, the Cursive Script is also more vivid than the Regular Script and the Official Script. Wang Xizhi's "Post of Lantin Foreword" is crowned the best Cursive Script in the history of Chinese calligraphy.

The Regular Script evolved from the Official Script and the Cursive Script and is the latest style to develop in Chinese history. It has been widely used since the Wei Dynasty (the period of Three Kingdoms, 220—280AD) and Jin Dynasty (265—420AD). In terms of calligraphic style it can be classified into Jin Regular Script, Wei Regular Script and Tang Regular Script, and in terms of size of characters into Big, Medium-sized and Small Regular Script.

Since the twentieth century, hard-tipped pen exerted a powerful impact replacing the brush. Hard-tip pen began to serve as the main writing tool in the field of Chinese calligraphy. The new pen, because of its practicality, greatly enhanced working and learning efficiency and is the most practical. As a result, the hard-tip calligraphy developed quickly. Broadly speaking, the characters written by the hard-tip pens made of different kinds of materials, like bamboo, wood, hard plastic, goose quill, bone, steel, or ball-point are called hard-tip characters, and the forms of Chinese characters with aesthetic values are called hard-tip pen calligraphy works.

The expressive style of hard-tip pen calligraphy are less than that of brush calligraphy, but in terms of structure, the two are almost identical. Both calligraphy styles are based on Chinese characters and follow the established rules concerning the stroke writing and order, components and structures. However, the brush calligraphers, because of the flexibility in maneuvering the brush, can produce more dynamic works. (The small script by Zhong Shaojing during Tang Dynasty can be adopted as a model for further study.)

Hard-tip calligraphy and brush calligraphy share many similarities due to the same writing content yet differ based on the distinct writing instruments used. Regardless, both styles are integral parts of the history of Chinese calligraphy and will remain a central component in Chinese culture.

2 | How to hold the pen
执笔方法

Han character, one of the oldest characters in the world, is a symbol for recording events. It evolved from pictogram into the square-shaped symbol composed of strokes. Han character is also called "square word," which consists of horizontal lines, vertical lines, down-left strokes, down-right strokes, hooks and so on. Writing follows a very precise rule constructed in upper-to-bottom structure, left-to-right structure and inner-to-outer structure inside squared space.

The pen should be held by the right hand and the paper pressed by the left hand. Paper should be placed straight on the table. The pen should be held in a 45-degree angle between the pen and the paper. Use three fingers to hold the pen and rest the forearms on the table naturally. The thumb and index finger bend naturally on both sides of the pen and hold tightly. The first joint of the middle finger pushes the pen inward, and the pen leans against the gap between the thumb and the index finger. The ring finger and the little finger bend naturally and lean against the back of the middle finger.

Keep the head and the body upright and stretch the arms. Put both feet solidly on the floor. Body should be relaxed.

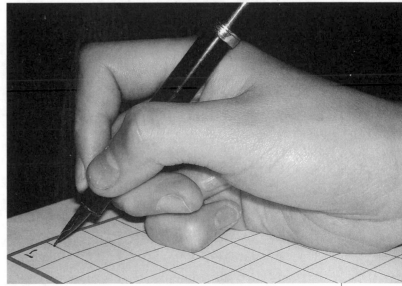

3 | Common vocabulary of strokes
常用笔画词汇

横 horizontal line	(一 *heng*)	斜捺 slanting down-right stroke
竖 vertical line	(丨 *shu*)	(乀 *xiena*)
撇 down-left stroke	(丿 *pie*)	平捺 flat down-right stroke
捺 down-right stroke	(乀 *na*)	(乀 *pingna*)
点 dot	(丶 *dian*)	斜提 slanting up-right tick (✓ *xieti*)
折 turn	(乛 *zhe*)	平提 flat up-right tick (一 *pingti*)
钩 hook	(亅 *gou*)	单立人 "single person" (亻 *danliren*)
提 tick	(一 *ti*)	双立人 "double person"
横撇 horizontal down-left stroke		(彳 *shuangliren*)
(乛 *hengpie*)		王字旁 "king" (王 *wang*)
横钩 horizontal hook	(一 *henggou*)	提土旁 "earth" (土 *tu*)
横折 horizontal turn	(乛 *hengzhe*)	两点水 "ice" (冫 *liangdianshui*)
横斜钩 horizontal slanting hook		三点水 "water" (氵 *sandianshui*)
(乚 *hengxiegou*)		宝盖 "roof" (宀 *baogai*)
横折钩 horizontal turning hook		秃宝盖 "over" (冖 *tubaogai*)
(亅 *hengzhegou*)		草字头 "grass" (艹 *cao*)
横折弯钩 horizontal turning curved		竹字头 "bamboo" (⺮ *zhu*)
hook (乚 *hengzhewangou*)		反文 "tap" (攵 *fanwen*)
悬针竖 vertical needle		欠字边 "lack" (欠 *qian*)
(丨 *xuanzhenshu*)		提手旁 "hand" (扌 *tishou*)
垂露竖 vertical dew	(丨 *chuilushu*)	木字旁 "tree" (木 *mu*)
竖折 vertical turn	(凵 *shuzhe*)	单耳旁 "single ear" (卩 *dan'er*)
竖提 vertical up-right tick	(亅 *shuti*)	双耳旁 "double ear" (阝 *shuang'er*)
竖弯 vertical curve	(乚 *shuwan*)	月字旁 "moon" (月 *yue*)
竖钩 vertical hook	(亅 *shugou*)	舟字旁 "boat" (舟 *zhou*)
竖弯钩 vertical curved hook		衣字旁 "clothes" (衤 *yi*)
(乚 *shuwangou*)		示字旁 "spirit" (礻 *shi*)
斜钩 slanting hook	(乀 *xiegou*)	立刀 "knife" (刂 *lidao*)
卧钩 lying hook	(乚 *wogou*)	寸字边 "inch" (寸 *cun*)
弯钩 curved hook	(亅 *wangou*)	人字头 "man" (人 *ren*)
撇折 down-left turn	(乚 *piezhe*)	春字头 "spring" (𡗗 *chun*)
撇点 down-left dot	(乚 *piedian*)	皿字底 "dish" (皿 *min*)
		四点底 "four dots" (灬 *sidian*)

Getting to know the grid " 田字格 *tianzege*" (a square grid divided into four cells)
认识田字格

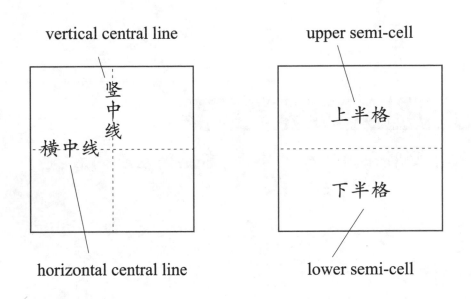

vertical central line

竖中线

横中线

horizontal central line

upper semi-cell

上半格

下半格

lower semi-cell

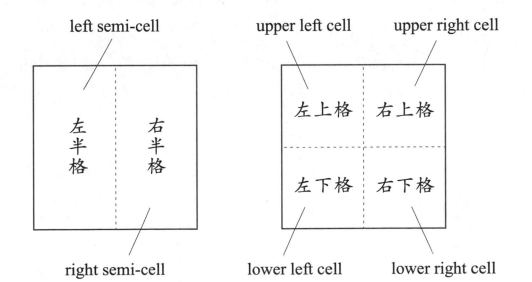

left semi-cell

左半格　右半格

right semi-cell

upper left cell　　upper right cell

左上格　右上格

左下格　右下格

lower left cell　　lower right cell

在田字格中写字要注意：

● 字要写在田字格的中间，不能偏左或偏右，也不能偏上或偏下。

● 字不能写得太小，也不能写得太大，四周应该留有一些空白。

When you write in cells, please notice:

The character should be written right in the middle of the square grid.

The character should be of the right size, leaving some blank spaces around.

5 | How to write horizontal strokes (一 *heng*)
横的写法

Stroke practice   笔画练习

long horizontal stroke

长 横

short horizontal stroke

短 横

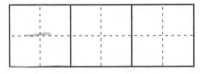

Single-character practice   单字练习

yī   一

èr   二

sān   一 二 三

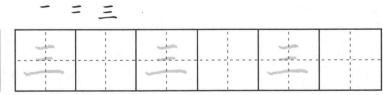

tiān   一 二 于 天

一	看	一	看	一	看		
二	听	二	听	二	听		
三	问	三	问	三	问		
白	天	白	天	白	天		
一	看	一	看	一	看		
二	听	二	听	二	听		
三	问	三	问	三	问		
白	天	白	天	白	天		

Stroke essentials 书写要点

When writing the horizontal line, the line is treated level with a slight slanting angle to the right. Gently start the stroke rightward, and gradually curve back to the left before lifting up the pen at the right end of the line.

The short horizontal line is written relatively short and is lower on the left and higher on the right.

The long horizontal line is written in a slight arc. When writing, the pen should be directed steadily. Learn to press down and lift up the pen.

Self-test exercise 自我测试

Practice writing the following characters on the four rows of grids provided. Check your work against the sample characters below.

一 二 三 天 一 二 三 天

6 | How to write vertical strokes(| *shu*)
竖的写法

Stroke practice   笔画练习

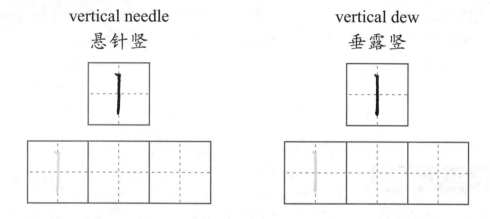

vertical needle
悬针竖

vertical dew
垂露竖

Single-character practice   单字练习

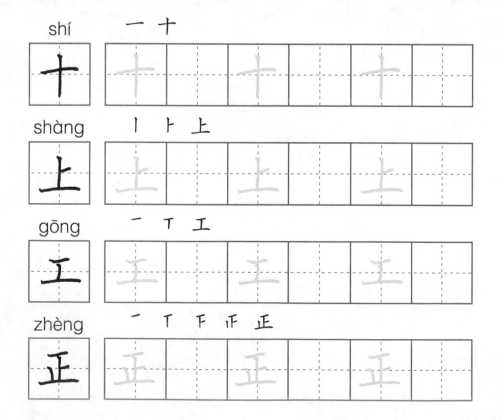

shí   一 十
十

shàng   丨 上 上
上

gōng   一 丁 工
工

zhèng   一 丁 下 正 正
正

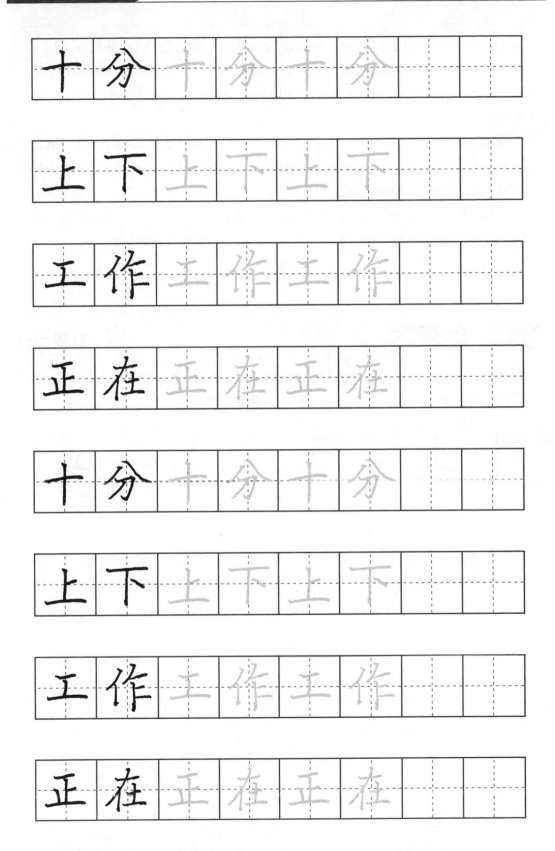

Stroke essentials 书写要点

The vertical line is the pillar of a character and is written upright and forceful to stabilize a character. When starting to write, first press down the pen to the lower right, then slightly bring up the pen and slowly press it downward to reach the bottom.

The vertical needle refers to the vertical line written with a pointy tip. It needs a revealed-tip which means to write it slightly and to bring the pen downward to reach the end without any force.

The vertical dew refers to the vertical line whose end is like a hanging dewdrop. The tip of the pen should turn a little bit upward before it is lifted up.

Self-test exercise 自我测试

Practice writing the following characters on the four rows of grids provided. Check your work against the sample characters below.

十 上 工 正 十 上 工 正

7 | How to write down-left strokes(ノ *pie*)
撇的写法

Stroke practice
笔画练习

flat down-left stroke	vertical down-left stroke	short down-left stroke	long down-left stroke
平　撇	竖　撇	短　撇	长　撇

   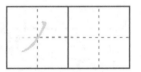

    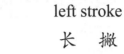

Single-character practice
单字练习

qiān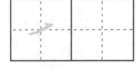

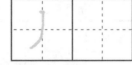

kāi

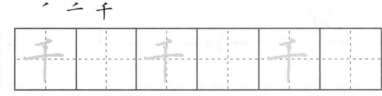

shēng

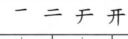

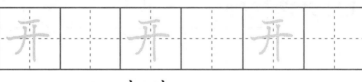

zuǒ

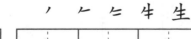

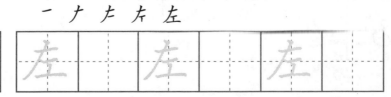

Practice Makes Perfect: Writing Chinese Characters 汉字书法经典指南

千米　千　米　千　米
开始　开　始　开　始
学生　学　生　学　生
左边　左　边　左　边
千米　千　米　千　米
开始　开　始　开　始
学生　学　生　学　生
左边　左　边　左　边

Stroke essentials 书写要点

The down-left stroke has four forms: the flat down-left stroke, the vertical down-left stroke, the short down-left stroke and the long down-left stroke.

The flat down-left stroke is horizontal and short with a pointy tip.

The vertical down-left stroke includes two steps, first to write a vertical line and then make a down-left stroke at a slow speed.

The short down-left stroke should be written forcefully and briskly.

The long down-left stroke is written slowly with a natural pointy-tip.

Mind the difference of the four forms.

Self-test exercise 自我测试

Practice writing the following characters on the four rows of grids provided. Check your work against the sample characters below.

千 开 生 左 千 开 生 左

Practice Makes Perfect: Writing Chinese Characters 汉字书法经典指南

8 | How to write down-right strokes (乀 *na*)
捺的写法

Stroke practice   笔画练习

slanting down-right stroke   flat down-right stroke

斜 捺   平 捺

   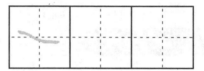

Single-character practice   单字练习

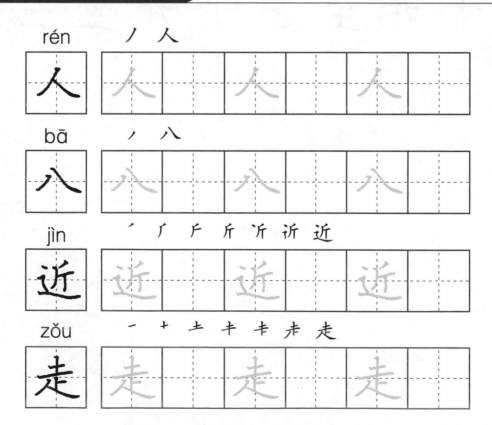

rén   丿 人

人

bā   丿 八

八

jìn   ´ 广 斤 斤 斤 近 近

近

zǒu   一 十 土 丰 走 走 走

走

There are two types of down-right strokes: the slanting down-right strokes and the flat down-right strokes. The down-right strokes are written long with a forked tail, which stretch out smoothly. Start the stroke from the top and move to the bottom right briskly. Pause briefly at the tail and finally make a rightward pointy tip with strength.

Start gently on the slanting down-right stroke, and bring the pen back a little bit to the opposite direction when starting a flat down-right stroke. The two strokes angle at different directions.

Self-test exercise 自我测试

Practice writing the following characters on the four rows of grids provided. Check your work against the sample characters below.

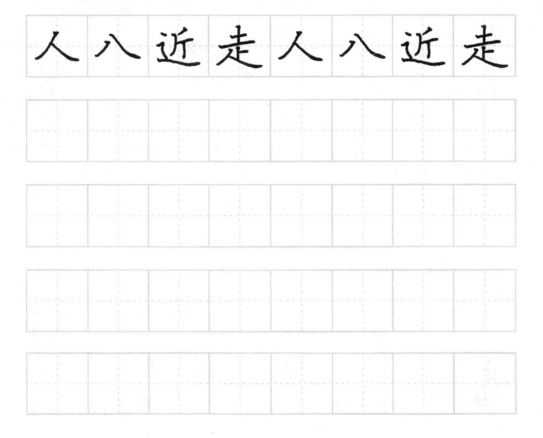

How to write dots (、 *dian*)
点的写法

Stroke practice　　　　　　　　　　笔画练习

leftward dot　　　　　　　　rightward dot
左　点　　　　　　　　　右　点

Single-character practice　　　　　　单字练习

shǎo　　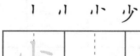

liù　　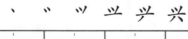
　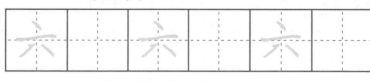

xìng　　

tóu　　

多	少	多	少	多	少		
六	个	六	个	六	个		
高	兴	高	兴	高	兴		
头	脑	头	脑	头	脑		
多	少	多	少	多	少		
六	个	六	个	六	个		
高	兴	高	兴	高	兴		
头	脑	头	脑	头	脑		

Practice Makes Perfect: Writing Chinese Characters　汉字书法经典指南

Stroke essentials 书写要点

The dot is characterized by a sharp head and a round ending. Pause the pen slightly at the end of a dot.

The leftward dot: start gently, press down the pen to the leftward, pause and then lift it up.

The rightward dot: press down the pen to the rightward slightly, pause and then return to the opposite direction before it is lifted up.

The writing of the leftward or the rightward dot is almost the same, but the motion of the pen is different. In order to balance the dot on the right, the dot on the left should make a slight rightward pointy tip. In most cases, the dot on the right is a little bit longer.

Self-test exercise 自我测试

Practice writing the following characters on the four rows of grids provided. Check your work against the sample characters below.

10 How to write turning strokes(乛 *zhe*)
折的写法

Stroke practice 笔画练习

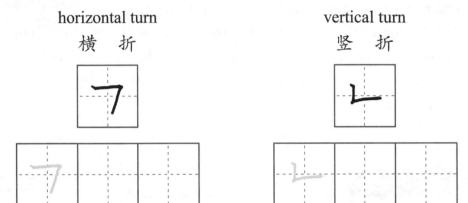

horizontal turn
横 折

vertical turn
竖 折

Single-character practice 单字练习

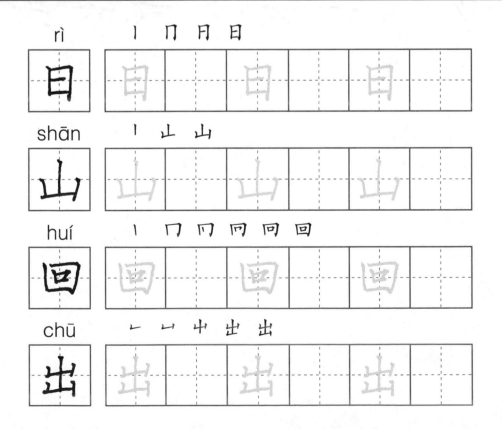

rì 日 丨 冂 月 日

shān 山 丨 山 山

huí 回 丨 冂 冋 冋 回 回

chū 出 乚 凵 屮 出 出

This stroke comes in two forms, the horizontal turn and vertical turn. The horizontal turn is the combination of a horizontal line and a vertical line with a turn at the joint. First write a horizontal line from left to right and pause briefly. Then write a vertical line to the lower left. The lifting up and pressing down are required at the turning point.

　　The vertical turn is the combination of a vertical line and a horizontal line. It can be divided into two kinds: square turn and round turn. The square turn is most frequently used. When the square turn is written, a vertical line is made first and then the pen is lifted up at the end, finally moved rightward.

Self-test exercise　　　　自我测试

Practice writing the following characters on the four rows of grids provided. Check your work against the sample characters below.

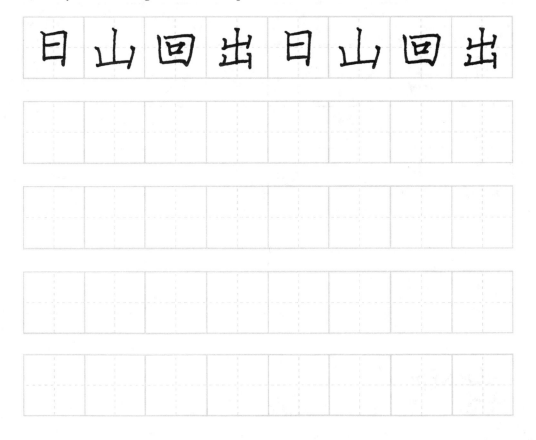

How to write hooks (亅 *gou*)
钩的写法

Stroke practice　　　　　　　　　　　　　　　　　　　　笔画练习

vertical hook　　　　　　　　　　　curved hook
竖　钩　　　　　　　　　　　　弯　钩

Single-character practice　　　　　　　　　　　　　　　单字练习

xiǎo　　亅 小 小

shǒu　　一 二 三 手

kě　　一 丁 丁 口 可

yú　　一 二 于

Stroke essentials 书写要点

This stroke comes in two forms, the vertical hook and curved hook. The vertical hook is similar to the vertical dew and the pen should press down in a leftward motion before lifting up, with the midfinger pushing the pen to the upper left. The hook should be made straightward.

When writing the curved hook, manage the pen slightly in an arc. The curved parts lie in the head and in the tail, and the central-part tends to be straight. The arc of the upper curve is relatively larger than that of the lower curve.

Self-test exercise 自我测试

Practice writing the following characters on the four rows of grids provided. Check your work against the sample characters below.

小	手	可	于	小	手	可	于

12 How to write up-right ticks(‑ *ti*)
提的写法

Stroke practice 笔画练习

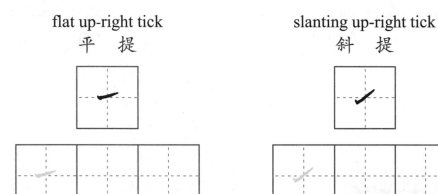

flat up-right tick
平 提

slanting up-right tick
斜 提

Single-character practice 单字练习

bān 班 一 二 ｆ 王 王 刬 珡 珡 班 班

jiāng 江 丶 丶 氵 汀 江 江

dǎ 打 一 扌 扌 扌 打

qiú 球 一 二 ｆ 王 王 玒 玒 玒 球 球

Stroke essentials 书写要点

There is little variation in this stroke. Press the tip of the pen firmly on paper, move upward briskly with a quick tip. When writing the up-right tick, the pen should move from the upper left to the lower right. Then hold the pen downward and turn to the upper right. Finally, the stroke should end with a pointy tip.

This stroke comes in two forms, the flat up-right tick and the slanting up-right tick. The two are similar, but the angle of lifting is different. The angle of the flat up-right tick is smaller than that of the slanting up-right tick.

Self-test exercise 自我测试

Practice writing the following characters on the four rows of grids provided. Check your work against the sample characters below.

班江打球班江打球

13 Vertical up-right tick(↓ *shuti*) and vertical curve(∟ *shuwan*)

竖提和竖弯

Stroke practice 笔画练习

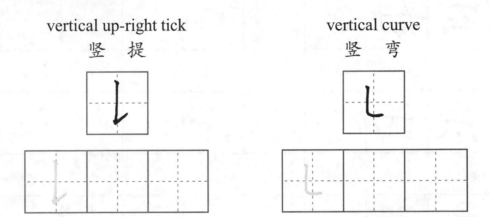

vertical up-right tick	vertical curve
竖 提	竖 弯

Single-character practice 单字练习

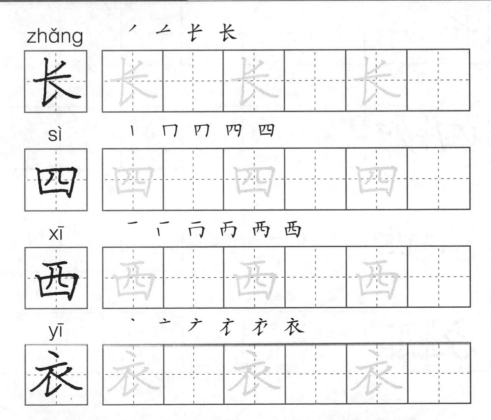

zhǎng 长 　ノ ←ー 丄 长

sì 四 　丨 冂 冃 四 四

xī 西 　一 丆 冚 两 西 西

yī 衣 　丶 亠 ナ 才 才 衣

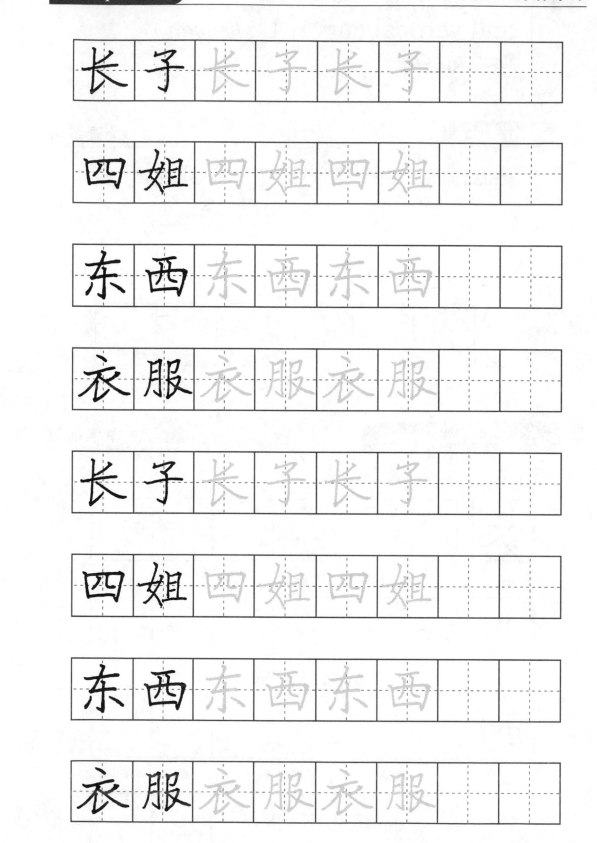

Make use of the cells to write the vertical up-right tick and the vertical curve stroke to sense their differences.

When writing the vertical up-right tick, the vertical line is made straight and the tick should be pointy at the tip. First press down and then lift up the pen at the turning point.

When writing the vertical curve, move the pen downward then rightward to make a circular and natural turn. Then continue to write a short horizontal line smoothly at one stretch. In most cases, the vertical line tends to be slightly longer than the horizontal one.

Self-test exercise 自我测试

Practice writing the following characters on the four rows of grids provided. Check your work against the sample characters below.

14 | Down-left turn (∠ *piezhe*) and down-left dot (㇗ *piedian*)
撇折和撇点

Stroke practice 　　　　　　　　　　　　　　　　笔画练习

down-left turn
撇 折

down-left dot
撇 点

Single-character practice 　　　　　　　　　　　单字练习

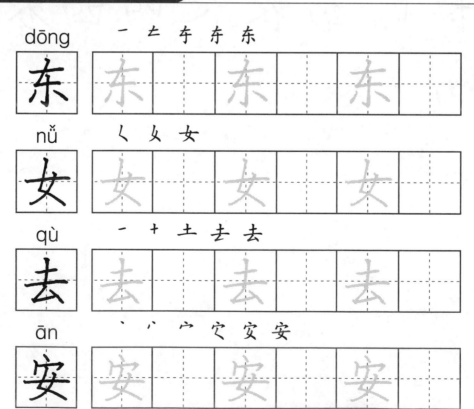

dōng　一 𠂉 𡆄 东 东
东

nǔ　㇗ 𡿨 女
女

qù　一 十 土 去 去
去

ān　丶 丷 宀 宀 安 安
安

⓮ Down-left turn（ㄥ *piezhe*）and down-left dot（ㄥ *piedian*）撇折和撇点

Stroke essentials 书写要点

This stroke is a combination of the down-left stroke and the horizontal stroke. Bring up the pen slightly upward in writing the turning stroke and lift up the pen at the turning point slightly then finish the rest of the stroke.

If the slanting stroke is long, the turning stroke is short and vice versa.

The down-left dot is a combination of the down-left stroke and long dot. The down-left strokes tends to be made slowly. When writing the dot, move the pen to the lower right and pressed a little harder before lifting up. In most cases, the length of the down-left stroke is the same as that of the dot.

Self-test exercise 自我测试

Practice writing the following characters on the four rows of grids provided. Check your work against the sample characters below.

东 女 去 安 东 女 去 安

15 Horizontal down-left stroke (ㄱ *hengpie*) and horizontal hook (乛 *henggou*) 横撇和横钩

Stroke practice　　　　　　　　　　　　　　　笔画练习

horizontal down-left stroke
横　撇

horizontal hook
横　钩

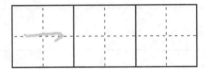

Single-character practice　　　　　　　　　　　单字练习

yòu　　ㄱ　又

又　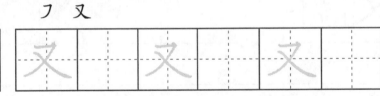

yú　　ノ　ク　ケ　㐅　召　曷　鱼　鱼

鱼　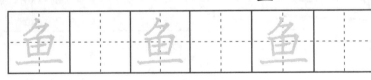

shuǐ　亅　刀　水　水

水　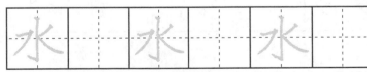

hàn　丶　冫　氵　沪　汉

汉　

Stroke essentials 书写要点

When writing the horizontal down-left stroke, the down-left stroke should be written a little bit longer. When writing the horizontal hook, the hook should be short and forceful. The sharp tip of the down-left stroke and the horizontal hook are revealed. The down-left stroke should be written faster than the hook.

Self-test exercise 自我测试

Practice writing the following characters on the four rows of grids provided. Check your work against the sample characters below.

又 鱼 水 汉 又 鱼 水 汉

16 | Lying hook (乚 *wogou*) and slanting hook (乀 *xiegou*)
卧钩和斜钩

Stroke practice

笔画练习

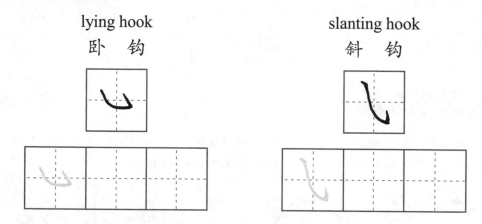

lying hook
卧 钩

slanting hook
斜 钩

Single-character practice

单字练习

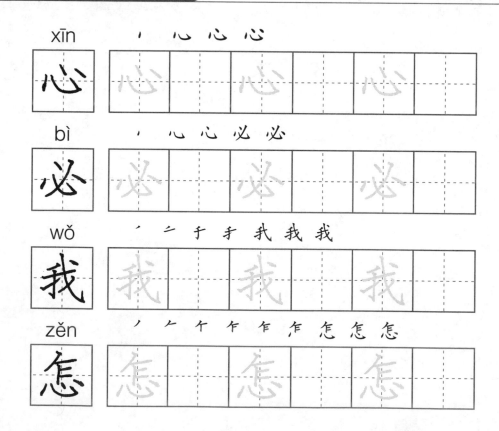

xīn

心

丶 心 心 心

bì

必

丶 心 心 必 必

wǒ

我

丿 一 于 手 我 我

zěn

怎

丿 ㇏ 午 午 作 乍 怎 怎 怎

小心　小心　小心

必须　必须　必须

我们　我们　我们

怎么　怎么　怎么

小心　小心　小心

必须　必须　必须

我们　我们　我们

怎么　怎么　怎么

The lying hook tends to be at the bottom of a character, and the slanting hook on the right.

    The lying hook is written with increasing strength from the upper left to the lower right in an arc. Hold the pen slightly and make a leftward hook.

    The slanting hook should be written from the upper left to the lower right. First hold the pen slightly and move to the lower right increasingly fast. The upper part should be straight and the lower part should end in a slight arc. Press down the pen when it moves to the end and make an upward hook.

Self-test exercise   自我测试

Practice writing the following characters on the four rows of grids provided. Check your work against the sample characters below.

17 Vertical curved hook (乚 *shuwangou*) and horizontal turning hook (㇆ *hengzhegou*) 竖弯钩和横折钩

Stroke practice 笔画练习

vertical curved hook
竖弯钩

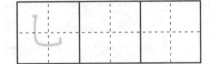

horizontal turning hook
横折钩

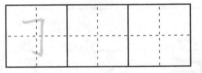

Single-character practice 单字练习

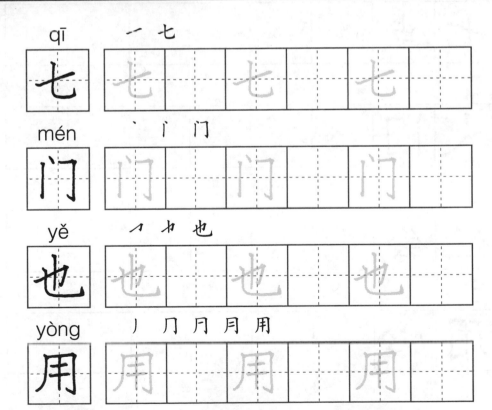

47

The vertical curved hook is usually made with a short vertical line and a long horizontal line at one stretch. Start from the lower left cell and turn rightward to write a horizontal line. Then make an upward hook. The turning point of this stroke should be written swiftly without any pause.

　　The horizontal turning hook is a combined stroke of a horizontal line and a vertical hook. The horizontal line is slightly shorter and the vertical hook longer. Pause briefly at the turning point.

Self-test exercise　　　　　　　　　　　　　　　　自我测试

Practice writing the following characters on the four rows of grids provided. Check your work against the sample characters below.

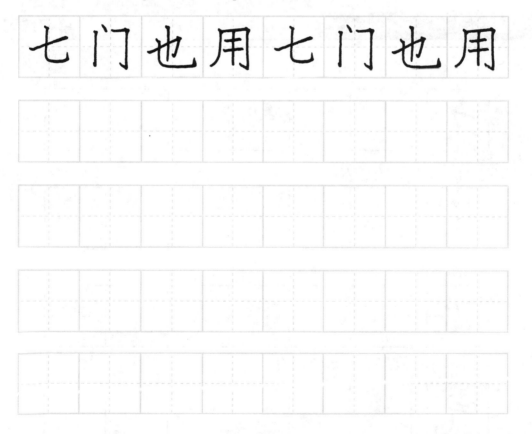

七 门 也 用 七 门 也 用

18 | Horizontal turning curved hook (乙 *hengzhewangou*) and horizontal slanting hook(飞 *hengxiegou*)
横折弯钩和横斜钩

horizontal turning curved hook
横折弯钩

horizontal slanting hook
横斜钩

Single-character practice 单字练习

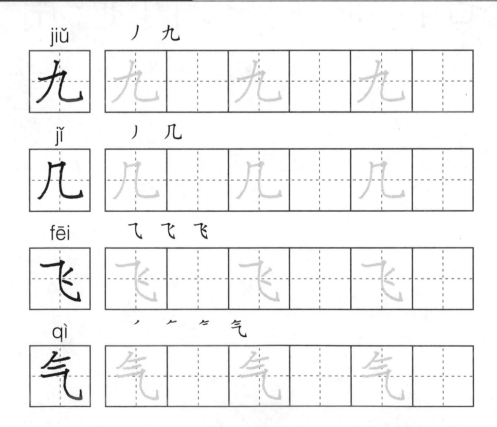

jiǔ ノ 九

jǐ ノ 几

fēi 乙 飞 飞

qì ノ 二 气 气

九 月 九 月 九 月

几 岁 几 岁 几 岁

飞 机 飞 机 飞 机

天 气 天 气 天 气

九 月 九 月 九 月

几 岁 几 岁 几 岁

飞 机 飞 机 飞 机

天 气 天 气 天 气

18 Horizontal turning curved hook（乙 *hengzhewangou*）and horizontal slanting hook（乙 *hengxiegou*）横折弯钩和横斜钩

Stroke essentials 书写要点

When writing the horizontal turning curved hook, first write a horizontal line low on the left and high on the right. Lift up and press down the pen when making a turning point. Then move the pen to the lower left and make a circular right turn. Pause briefly at the end and lift up the pen to make an upward hook.

The horizontal slanting hook is a combination of a horizontal line and a slanting hook. When writing, extend the hook to the right. Slant the horizontal line briefly. Make a bigger arc than the single slanting hook.

Self-test exercise 自我测试

Practice writing the following characters on the four rows of grids provided. Check your work against the sample characters below.

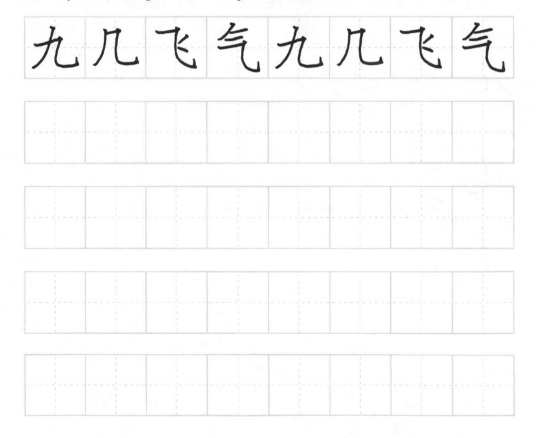

19 | Single characters I
独体字（一）

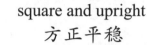

Getting to know the characters 认识字形

flat horizontal line and straight vertical line
横平竖直

square and upright
方正平稳

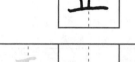 

Single-character practice 单字练习

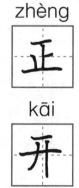

zhèng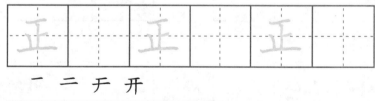

正

kāi

开

zhǔ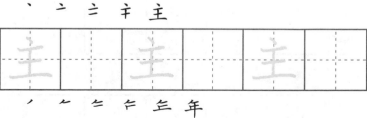

主

nián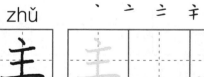

年

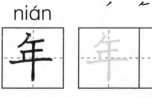

The single characters look easy but they are not so easy to write well.

First, follow the structural rule of "flat horizontal line and straight vertical line, square and upright."

A square single character has a flat horizontal line and straight vertical line so that the character is well-balanced.

While writing, learn to observe and compare. Slow down a little bit and mind the lifting and pressing of the pen to make the strokes refined and elegant.

The character "正": Try to observe which strokes of the character lies in the middle and which strokes are longer.

Self-test exercise 自我测试

Practice writing the following characters on the four rows of grids provided. Check your work against the sample characters below.

正 开 主 年 正 开 主 年

20 | Single characters II
独体字（二）

Getting to know the characters　　　　　　　　认识字形

highlighting the main strokes
突出主笔

making a distinction between the important strokes and lesser ones 主次分明

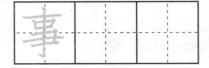

Single-character practice　　　　　　　　单字练习

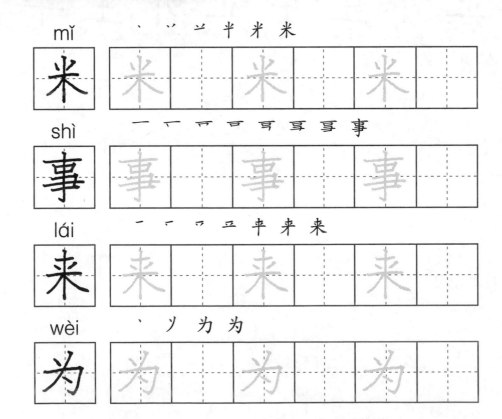

Stroke essentials 书写要点

Follow the rule of highlighting the main stroke.

When writing the single characters of this part, try to highlight the main strokes and stretch them out so that a distinction can be made among all the strokes.

The character "米": The main stroke is the vertical line. The first and second dots should point at the mid vertical line from the two sides; the third and the fourth strokes, which are the horizontal and vertical lines, are written in the center. The fifth and sixth strokes, which are down-left stroke and down-right stroke, should stretch out from the middle.

Self-test exercise 自我测试

Practice writing the following characters on the four rows of grids provided. Check your work against the sample characters below.

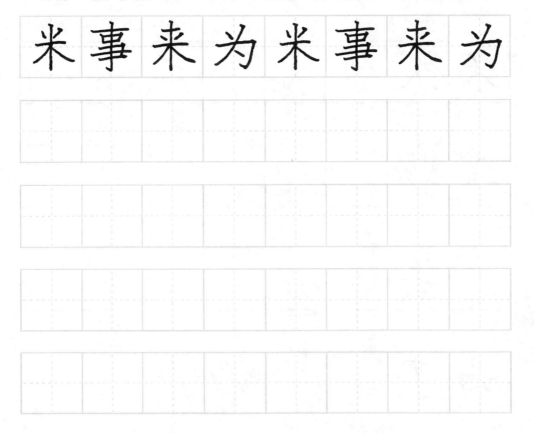

Practice Makes Perfect: Writing Chinese Characters 汉字书法经典指南

21 Radicals of "single person"(亻 *danliren*) and "double person"(彳 *shuangliren*)

单立人和双立人

Radical practice

偏旁练习

radical of "single person"

单立人

radical of "double person"

双立人

Single-character practice

单字练习

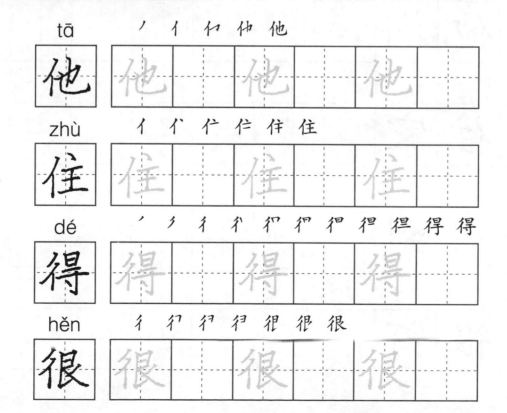

tā 他 ノ 亻 仆 他 他

zhù 住 亻 亻 仁 住 住 住

dé 得 ノ ク 彳 彳 彳 彳 彳 得 得

hěn 很 彳 彳 彳 彳 很 很

他们 | 他 | 们 | 他 | 们 | | |

住家 | 住 | 家 | 住 | 家 | | |

得到 | 得 | 到 | 得 | 到 | | |

很好 | 很 | 好 | 很 | 好 | | |

他们 | 他 | 们 | 他 | 们 | | |

住家 | 住 | 家 | 住 | 家 | | |

得到 | 得 | 到 | 得 | 到 | | |

很好 | 很 | 好 | 很 | 好 | | |

Practice Makes Perfect: Writing Chinese Characters 汉字书法经典指南

When writing the radical of "single person," make sure the down-left stroke is not too flat or too straight. Start the vertical line from the middle of the down-left stroke and it should be of the same length as the down-left stroke.

When writing the "double person," the first down-left stroke is written short and the second down-left stroke slightly longer. Make them parallel. The starting point of these two down-left strokes should be perpendicular. Do not make the vertical line too long.

Self-test exercise 自我测试

Practice writing the following characters on the four rows of grids provided. Check your work against the sample characters below.

他 住 得 很 他 住 得 很

22 Radicals of "king"(王 *wang*) and "earth"(土 *tu*)

王字旁和提土旁

Radical practice
偏旁练习

radical of "king"
王字旁

radical of "earth"
提土旁

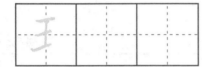

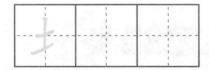

Single-character practice
单字练习

xiàn
现
一 二 三 丰 王 玑 玑 现 现

qiú
球
王 王 玎 玎 玎 玎 球 球

kuài
块
一 十 土 圡 圡 块 块

chéng
城
土 圠 圠 圻 城 城 城

Stroke essentials 书写要点

The radicals of "king" and "earth." When "king" is arranged as a left radical, the first two horizontal lines should be short. The vertical line is written in the middle. The last horizontal line should be written as an up-right tick.

When writing the radical of "earth ," first slant the short horizontal line. Write the vertical line across the horizontal line. Then make a straight and forceful up-right tick at the bottom.

Mind that the last strokes of these two radicals are ticks rather than horizontal lines.

Self-test exercise 自我测试

Practice writing the following characters on the four rows of grids provided. Check your work against the sample characters below.

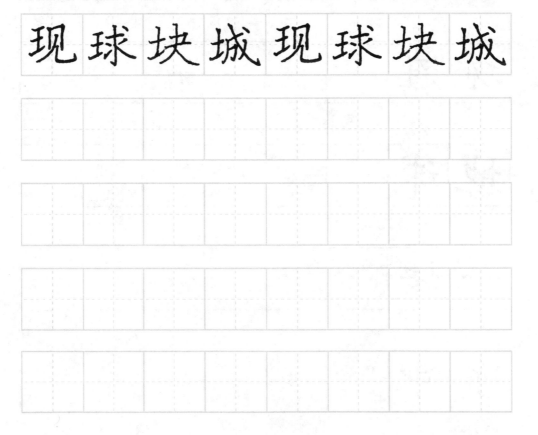

Radicals of "ice" (冫 *liangdianshui*) and **"water"** (氵 *sandianshui*) (two dots and three dots)　两点水和三点水

Radical practice 偏旁练习

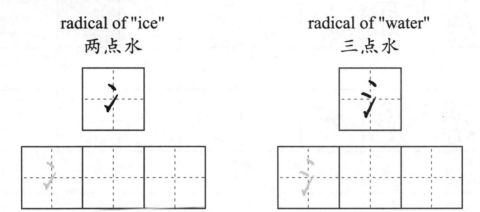

radical of "ice"　　　　　　　　　radical of "water"
两点水　　　　　　　　　　　　　三点水

Single-character practice 单字练习

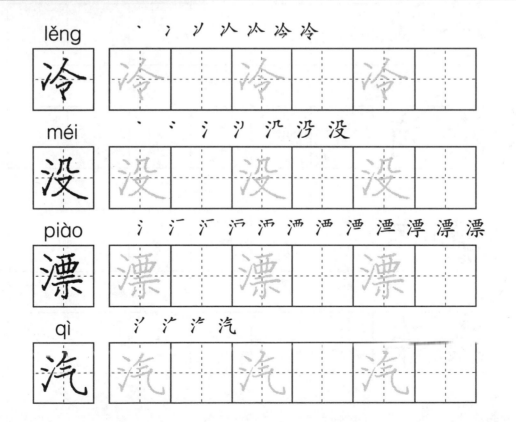

lěng　　、冫丿八冫冷冷
冷

méi　　、冫氵汐沿没
没

piào　　氵氵氵沪沪沪沪沪漂漂漂
漂

qì　　氵氵氵汽
汽

Practice Makes Perfect: Writing Chinese Characters 汉字书法经典指南

These two radicals are usually narrow and on the left of a character.

When the radical of ice is written, the upper and underneath strokes should mirror each other at the appropriate distance. Mind that the right and left strokes of the whole character are inserted independently of one another and do not cross.

When writing the radical of "water," first make a rightward dot, then slant the second rightward dot slightly to the left, and finally make an up-right tick. The three strokes should be in the left half of the character.

Self-test exercise 自我测试

Practice writing the following characters on the four rows of grids provided. Check your work against the sample characters below.

冷 没 漂 汽 冷 没 漂 汽

24 | Radicals of "over"(冖 *tubaogai*) and "roof "(宀 *baogai*)

秃宝盖和宝盖

Radical practice

radical of "over"
秃宝盖

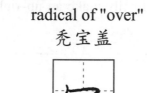

radical of "roof "
宝盖

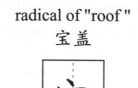

Single-character practice

xiě

jūn
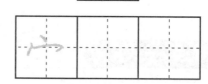

zì

shì

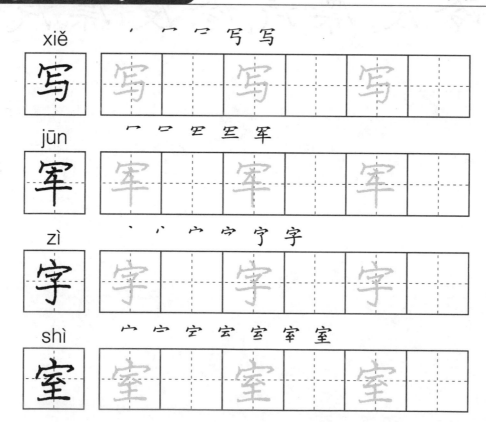

写	字	写	字	写	字		

军	人	军	人	军	人		

字	体	字	体	字	体		

室	外	室	外	室	外		

写	字	写	字	写	字		

军	人	军	人	军	人		

字	体	字	体	字	体		

室	外	室	外	室	外		

Stroke essentials 书写要点

When writing the radical of "over," first write a vertical dot. Make sure the dot is not too long that it becomes a short down-left stroke. Move the pen leftward. Pause the pen briefly at the turning point and make a hook quickly.

When writing the radical of "roof ," first write a dot in the middle of the upper semi-cell. Repeat the steps of writing the radical of "over."

Self-test exercise 自我测试

Practice writing the following characters on the four rows of grids provided. Check your work against the sample characters below.

25 Radicals of "grass" (艹 *cao*) and "bamboo" (竹 *zhu*)

草字头和竹字头

Radical practice

偏旁练习

radical of "grass"
草字头

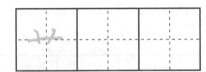

radical of "bamboo"
竹字头

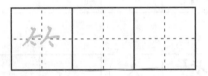

Single-character practice

单字练习

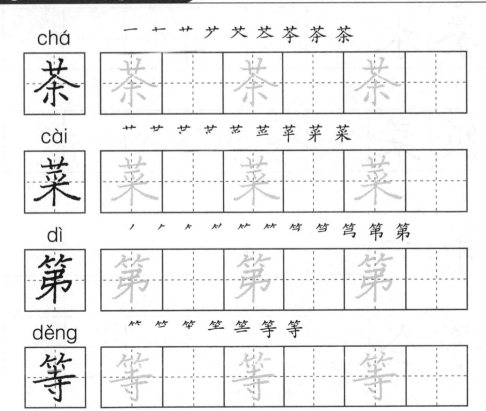

chá 茶 — 一 十 卄 艹 艾 艾 苓 茶 茶

cài 菜 — 艹 艹 艹 艹 芸 苙 苙 苙 菜

dì 第 — 丿 ⺇ ⺮ ⺮ ⺮ ⺮ 竻 笃 笃 第 第

děng 等 — 竻 竻 竻 竺 竺 等 等

Practice Makes Perfect: Writing Chinese Characters 汉字书法经典指南

Stroke essentials 书写要点

When writing the radical of "grass," write the short vertical line and down-left stroke to the middle. The horizontal line crosses at one-third of these two strokes from the bottom. The short vertical line and down-left stroke should be slightly apart at the top and relatively closer to each other at the bottom. The order of the strokes is horizontal line-vertical line-down-left stroke; or vertical line-horizontal line-down-left stroke.

The radical of bamboo should be written straight and make the left and the right part be well-balanced. The third stroke and the last stroke are dots, which can not be written like vertical line or vertical hook.

Self-test exercise 自我测试

Practice writing the following characters on the four rows of grids provided. Check your work against the sample characters below.

茶 菜 第 等 茶 菜 第 等

26 | Radicals of "tap" (攵 *fanwen*) and "lack" (欠 *qian*)
反文和欠字边

Radical practice   偏旁练习

radical of "tap"   radical of "lack"

反文   欠字边

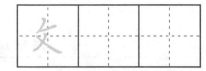

Single-character practice   单字练习

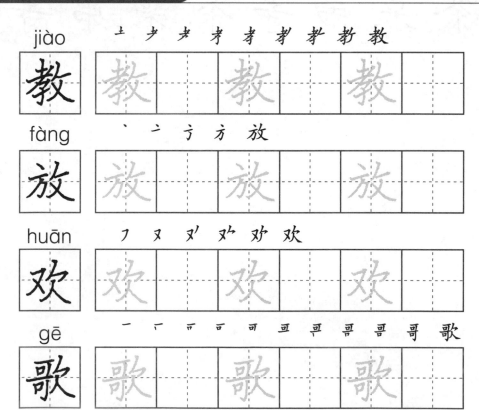

jiào 教

fàng 放

huān 欢

gē 歌

Stroke essentials   书写要点

The radical of "tap" consists of four steps. The first down-left stroke and second horizontal line should not be too long. The short horizontal line should be halfway down the first stroke. The third vertical down-left stroke should start from the center-left part, move vertically to the half and make a down-left stroke to the bottom left. Stretch out the foot of the down-right stroke.

The radical of "lack" starts with the short down-left stroke. The second horizontal hook starts from the end of the first stroke. The long down-left stroke is slanted to the left. The last down-right stroke is stretched out.

Self-test exercise   自我测试

Practice writing the following characters on the four rows of grids provided. Check your work against the sample characters below.

教	放	欢	歌	教	放	欢	歌

27 Radicals of "hand"(扌 *tishou*) and "tree"(木 *mu*)
提手旁和木字旁

Radical practice   偏旁练习

radical of "hand"
提手旁

radical of "tree"
木字旁

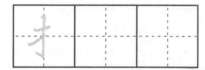

Single-character practice   单字练习

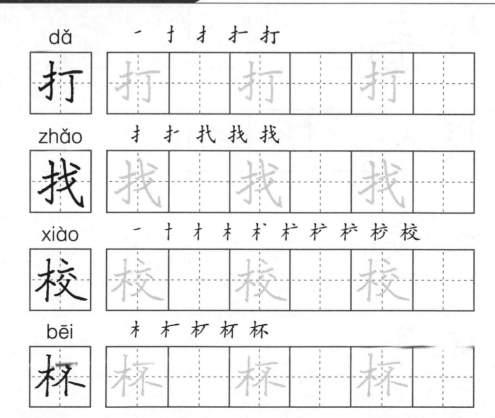

These two radicals should be written long and thin with a width that takes up one-third of the whole character. Mind the intersections of the strokes.

"Hand": Slant the short horizontal line slightly. Straighten the vertical hook to make it a little bit longer and cross the horizontal line. The up-right tick intersects with the vertical hook.

"Tree": Slant the short horizontal line slightly and straighten the vertical line. The point of the down-left stroke is higher than the end of the vertical line. The down-right stroke is shortened into a dot, whose starting point is below the starting point of the down-left stroke.

Self-test exercise　　　　　　　　　　　　　　　　自我测试

Practice writing the following characters on the four rows of grids provided. Check your work against the sample characters below.

打 找 校 杯 打 找 校 杯

28 Radicals of "single ear" (卩 *dan'er*) and "double ear" (阝 *shuang'er*)

单耳旁和双耳旁

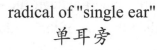

Radical practice　　　　　　　　　　　　　　　　　偏旁练习

radical of "single ear"　　　　　　　　　radical of "double ear"
　　　单耳旁　　　　　　　　　　　　　　　双耳旁

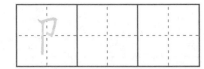　　　　　　　　

Single-character practice　　　　　　　　　　　　单字练习

què　却　一 十 土 去 去 刧 却

yuàn　院　丁 阝 阝 阝 阝 陀 陀 院 院

dōu　都　一 十 土 耂 耂 者 者 都

nà　那　刁 刁 刕 那 那

了 却
医 院
都 是
那 儿
了 却
医 院
都 是
那 儿

In order to write these two radicals well, practice the writing of horizontal turning hook and horizontal turning curved hook.

When writing the radical of "single ear," the upper part of this radical is wide at the top and narrow at the bottom. This radical is usually on the right of the character. The vertical line should be slightly longer and straight.

"Double ear": this radical is on the left of the character, the horizontal down-left curved hook should be written smaller; when it is on the right, it should be written bigger and the vertical line should be slightly longer.

Self-test exercise   自我测试

Practice writing the following characters on the four rows of grids provided. Check your work against the sample characters below.

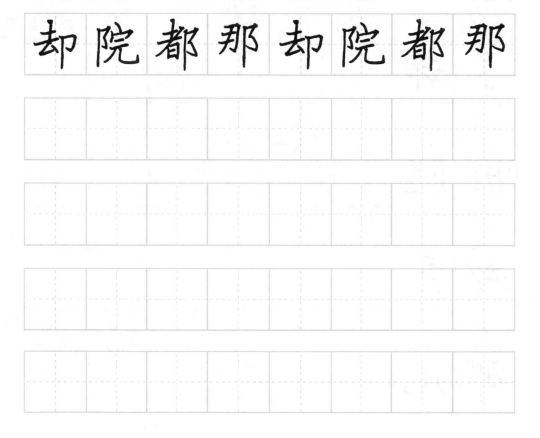

29 Radicals of "moon"(月 *yue*) and "boat" (舟 *zhou*)

月字旁和舟字旁

Radical practice   偏旁练习

radical of "moon" 月字旁	radical of "boat" 舟字旁
月	舟

Single-character practice   单字练习

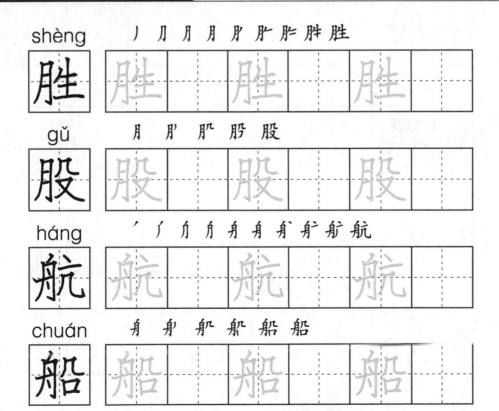

shèng 丿 刀 月 月 肝 胪 肸 胜 胜
胜   胜   胜   胜

gǔ 月 月 肝 股 股
股   股   股   股

háng ノ 丿 月 月 舟 舟 舟 舟 舩 航
航   航   航   航

chuán 舟 舟 舩 船 船 船
船   船   船   船

Stroke essentials 书写要点

Radicals of "moon" and "boat" take up only one-third of the whole character.

The radical of "moon" consists of four steps. It is slightly longer. The first is a vertical down-left stroke. The mid two short horizontal lines are slightly higher in position, taking the shape of being tight at the top and loose at the bottom. There should be a little space on the right end of the short horizontal lines to make the character elegant.

The radical of "boat" consists of six strokes, taking the shape of being tight at the top and loose at the bottom. The first stroke is a short down-left stroke, and second is a vertical down-left stroke. The central horizontal line is changed into a right-up tick.

Self-test exercise 自我测试

Practice writing the following characters on the four rows of grids provided. Check your work against the sample characters below.

胜 股 航 船 胜 股 航 船

30 | Radicals of "spirit"(礻 *shi*) and "clothes"(衤 *yi*)
示字旁和衣字旁

Radical practice   偏旁练习

radical of "spirit"   radical of "clothes"

示字旁   衣字旁

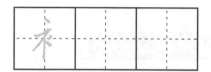

Single-character practice   单字练习

Stroke essentials
书写要点

The radical of "spirit" consists of four strokes. The first one is the dot at the side and the second one is the short horizontal down-left stroke, which keeps a certain distance away from the dot. The third one is the vertical "dew," which is aligned with the dot at the side. The last stroke of "dot" is started near the starting point of the vertical line. Mind the variation of the two dots.

The writing of the radical of "clothes" is similar to that of the "spirit." The only difference lies in the lower position of the last two strokes, the two dots, which are in coordination with each other.

Mind the difference of these two radicals.

Self-test exercise
自我测试

Practice writing the following characters on the four rows of grids provided. Check your work against the sample characters below.

31 | Radicals of "knife"(刂 *lidao*) and "inch"(寸 *cun*)

立刀和寸字边

Radical practice
偏旁练习

radical of "knife"
立刀

radical of "inch"
寸字边

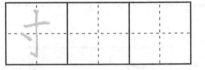

Single-character practice
单字练习

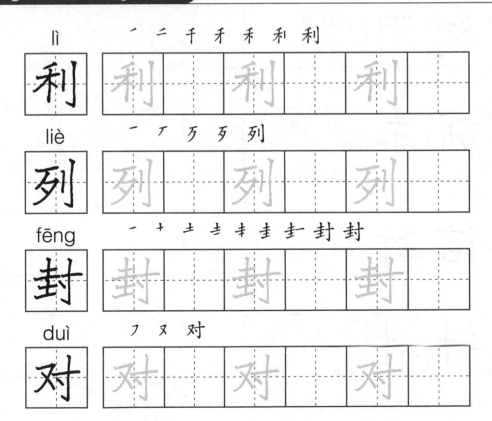

lì 一 二 千 千 禾 利 利
利

liè 一 ア 歹 歹 列
列

fēng 一 十 土 圡 丰 圭 圭 封 封
封

duì フ 又 对
对

利用　利用　利用

列车　列车　列车

信封　信封　信封

针对　针对　针对

利用　利用　利用

列车　列车　列车

信封　信封　信封

针对　针对　针对

Stroke essentials

These two radicals are relatively simple but have to be written elegantly. Carefully observe the characters with these two radicals and get to know the rules of writing by comparison and analysis of the differences of the two strokes. Practice writing the characters with these two radicals repeatedly.

When the "knife" and "inch" are used as right radicals, the left part of the character should not be too long nor go beyond the vertical hook.

The vertical hook of these two radicals should be written long and thin with a slight arc to the left in the central part.

Self-test exercise

Practice writing the following characters on the four rows of grids provided. Check your work against the sample characters below.

利 列 封 对 利 列 封 对

Radicals of "man" (人 *ren*) and "spring" (夫 *chun*)

人字头和春字头

Radical practice
偏旁练习

radical of "man"
人字头

radical of "spring"
春字头

Single-character practice
单字练习

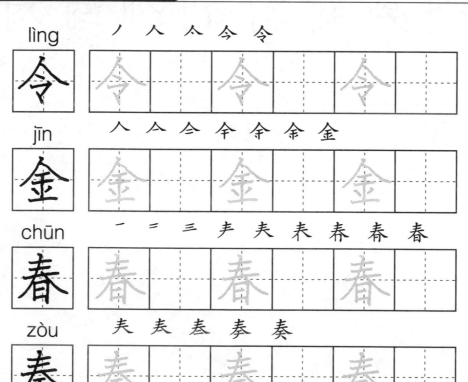

lìng
ノ 人 △ 今 令
令

jīn
人 △ 今 全 全 金 金
金

chūn
一 二 三 声 夫 未 春 春 春
春

zòu
夫 表 表 奏 奏
奏

Stroke essentials

In writing the radical of "man," stretch out the down-left a[nd] smoothly. The starting point of the down-right stroke is sl[...] down-left stroke. Make a pointy tip at the end of the down-ri[ght] pen. Mind the angle of these two strokes.

When writing the radical of "spring," tighten the three l[...] equal space between each other and do not make them too [...] lines too long. The starting point of the down-right stroke s[...] part of the third horizontal line rather than cross the down-le[ft]

Self-test exercise   自我测试

Practice writing the following characters on the four rows of grids provided. Check your work against the sample characters below.

令 金 春 奏 令 金 春 奏

33 Radicals of "dish"(皿 *min*) and "four dots"(灬 *sidian*)

皿字底和四点底

Radical practice   偏旁练习

radical of "dish"   radical of "four dots"
皿字底   四点底

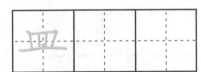

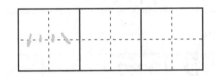

Single-character practice   单字练习

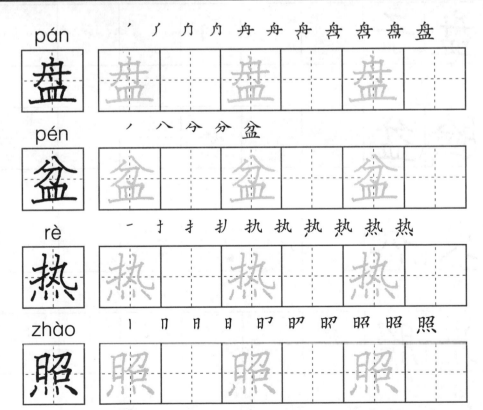

pán

盘 ´ ㇒ 几 㐅 舟 舟 舟 舟 舟 盘 盘

pén

盆 ´ 八 分 分 盆

rè

热 一 亅 扌 扚 执 执 执 热 热 热

zhào

照 丨 冂 日 日 日' 昭 昭 照 照 照

The radical of "dish" consists of five strokes. Slant the left vertical line and horizontal turn to the central line slightly. The shape of the radical is slightly wider at the top than at the bottom. It should be written relatively wide and flat. The last horizontal line should be a bit longer to support the upper part.

The radical of "four dots" should be written flat and wide evenly. The four dots are written from left to right. The outer two dots are longer and the inner two dots are shorter. The radical should be written narrow on the top and wide at the bottom.

Self-test exercise 自我测试

Practice writing the following characters on the four rows of grids provided. Check your work against the sample characters below.

盆 盆 热 照 盆 盆 热 照

34 | Left-to-right structure
左右结构

Structure practice 结构练习

left-right symmetry	wide left and narrow right	narrow left and wide right
左右等宽	左宽右窄	左窄右宽

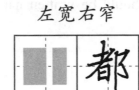  

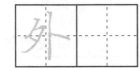 

Single-character practice 单字练习

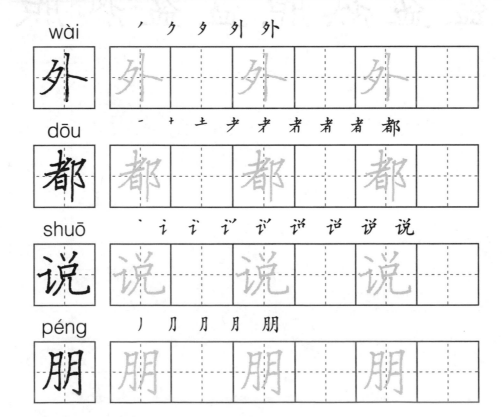

Stroke essentials 书写要点

There are three types of left-to-right structure: （1）left and right parts are of equal size, for example, the character "外"; （2）a large left and a small right, for example, the character "都"; （3）a small left and a large right, for example, the character "说."

In order to write a balanced and beautiful Chinese character, arrange the strokes carefully. Before writing, look at the layout of a character and the proportion of the left and right parts. While writing, be careful that some strokes cross through and some do not.

Self-test exercise 自我测试

Practice writing the following characters on the four rows of grids provided. Check your work against the sample characters below.

35 | Top-to-bottom structure
上下结构

Structure practice 结构练习

wide-flat top and narrow-long bottom
上宽扁下窄长

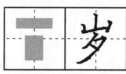

narrow-long top and wide-flat bottom
上窄长下宽扁

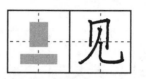

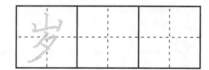

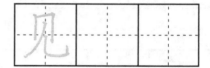

Single-character practice 单字练习

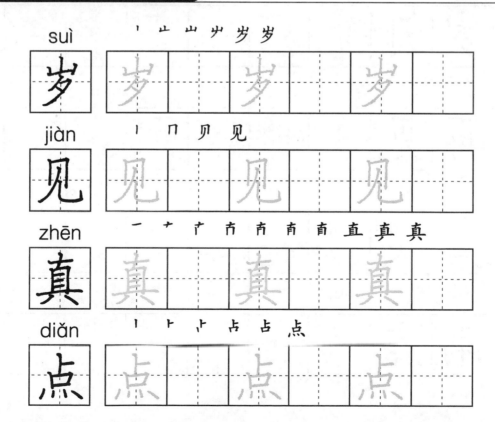

suì — 岁 (丨 屮 屮 屵 岁 岁)

jiàn — 见 (丨 冂 贝 见)

zhēn — 真 (一 十 广 市 市 甫 肯 直 真 真)

diǎn — 点 (丨 卜 占 占 占 点)

Stroke essentials 书写要点

There are six types of top-to-bottom structures: (1) a wide top and a narrow bottom; (2) a narrow top and a wide bottom; (3) a wide, flat top and a narrow, long bottom; (4) a narrow, long top and a wide, flat bottom; (5) a loose top and a tight bottom; and (6) a tight top and a loose bottom. Control the layout of the top and bottom properly.

When writing the top-to-bottom characters, first look at the layout of the character. Then decide which of the six structures the character should build upon.

Self-test exercise 自我测试

Practice writing the following characters on the four rows of grids provided. Check your work against the sample characters below.

岁 见 真 点 岁 见 真 点

HSK(Chinese Proficiency Test) Vocabularies
附:HSK(汉语水平考试)词汇

Practice Makes Perfect: Writing Chinese Characters 汉字书法经典指南

A

1. ā yí 阿姨
2. a 啊
3. ǎi 矮
4. ài 爱
5. ài hào 爱好
6. ān jìng 安静

B

7. bā 八
8. bǎ 把
9. bà ba 爸爸
10. ba 吧
11. bái 白
12. bǎi 百
13. bān 班
14. bān 搬
15. bàn 半
16. bàn fǎ 办法
17. bàn gōng shì 办公室
18. bāng máng 帮忙
19. bāng zhù 帮助
20. bāo 包
21. bǎo 饱
22. bào zhǐ 报纸
23. bēi zi 杯子
24. běi fāng 北方
25. běi jīng 北京
26. bèi 被
27. běn 本
28. bí zi 鼻子
29. bǐ 比
30. bǐ jiào 比较

31. bǐ sài 比赛
32. bì xū 必须
33. biàn huà 变化
34. biǎo shì 表示
35. biǎo yǎn 表演
36. bié 别
37. bié rén 别人
38. bīn guǎn 宾馆
39. bīng xiāng 冰箱
40. bú kè qi 不客气
41. bù 不

C

42. cái 才
43. cài 菜
44. cài dān 菜单
45. cān jiā 参加

46. cǎo 草
47. céng 层
48. chá 茶
49. chà 差
50. cháng 长
51. chàng gē 唱歌
52. chāo shì 超市
53. chèn shān 衬衫
54. chéng jì 成绩
55. chéng shì 城市
56. chī 吃
57. chí dào 迟到
58. chū 出
59. chū xiàn 出现
60. chū zū chē 出租车
61. chú fáng 厨房
62. chú le 除了

chuān 63. 穿	dāng rán 81. 当然	dōng xi 101. 东西	èr 119. 二
chuán 64. 船	dào 82. 到	dōng 102. 冬	**F**
chūn 65. 春	de 83. 地	dǒng 103. 懂	
cí yǔ 66. 词语	de 84. 的	dòng wù 104. 动物	fā shāo 120. 发烧
cì 67. 次	de 85. 得	dōu 105. 都	fā xiàn 121. 发现
cōng míng 68. 聪明	dēng 86. 灯	dú 106. 读	fàn guǎn 122. 饭馆
cóng 69. 从	děng 87. 等	duǎn 107. 短	fāng biàn 123. 方便
cuò 70. 错	dī 88. 低	duàn 108. 段	fáng jiān 124. 房间
D	dì di 89. 弟弟	duàn liàn 109. 锻炼	fàng 125. 放
	dì fang 90. 地方	duì 110. 对	fàng xīn 126. 放心
dǎ diàn huà 71. 打电话	dì tiě 91. 地铁	duì bu qǐ 111. 对不起	fēi cháng 127. 非常
dǎ lán qiú 72. 打篮球	dì tú 92. 地图	duō 112. 多	fēi jī 128. 飞机
dǎ sǎo 73. 打扫	dì yī 93. 第一	duō me 113. 多么	fēn 129. 分
dǎ suàn 74. 打算	diǎn 94. 点	duō shao 114. 多少	fēn zhōng 130. 分钟
dà 75. 大	diàn nǎo 95. 电脑	**E**	fú wù yuán 131. 服务员
dà jiā 76. 大家	diàn shì 96. 电视		fù jìn 132. 附近
dài 77. 带	diàn tī 97. 电梯	è 115. 饿	fù xí 133. 复习
dān xīn 78. 担心	diàn yǐng 98. 电影	ér qiě 116. 而且	**G**
dàn gāo 79. 蛋糕	diàn zǐ yóu jiàn 99. 电子邮件	ér zi 117. 儿子	
dàn shì 80. 但是	dōng 100. 东	ěr duo 118. 耳朵	gān jìng 134. 干净

gǎn 135. 敢	guā fēng 154. 刮 风	hē 172. 喝	huì 192. 会
gǎn mào 136. 感 冒	guān 155. 关	hé 173. 和	huì yì 193. 会 议
gāng cái 137. 刚 才	guān xì 156. 关 系	hé 174. 河	huǒ chē zhàn 194. 火 车 站
gāo 138. 高	guān xīn 157. 关 心	hēi 175. 黑	huò zhě 195. 或 者
gāo xìng 139. 高 兴	guān yú 158. 关 于	hēi bǎn 176. 黑 板	
gào su 140. 告 诉	guì 159. 贵	hěn 177. 很	**J**
gē ge 141. 哥 哥	guó jiā 160. 国 家	hóng 178. 红	jī chǎng 196. 机 场
gè 142. 个	guǒ zhī 161. 果 汁	hòu miàn 179. 后 面	jī dàn 197. 鸡 蛋
gěi 143. 给	guò qù 162. 过 去	hù zhào 180. 护 照	jī hū 198. 几 乎
gēn 144. 跟	guo 163. 过	huā 181. 花	jī huì 199. 机 会
gēn jù 145. 根 据	**H**	huā yuán 182. 花 园	jí 200. 极
gèng 146. 更		huà 183. 画	jǐ 201. 几
gōng gòng 147. 公 共	hái 164. 还	huài 184. 坏	jì de 202. 记 得
qì chē 汽 车	hái shì 165. 还 是	huān yíng 185. 欢 迎	jì jié 203. 季 节
gōng jīn 148. 公 斤	hái zi 166. 孩 子	huán 186. 还	jiā 204. 家
gōng sī 149. 公 司	hài pà 167. 害 怕	huán jìng 187. 环 境	jiǎn chá 205. 检 查
gōng yuán 150. 公 园	Hàn yǔ 168. 汉 语	huàn 188. 换	jiǎn dān 206. 简 单
gōng zuò 151. 工 作	hǎo 169. 好	huáng 189. 黄	jiàn 207. 件
gǒu 152. 狗	hǎo chī 170. 好 吃	huí 190. 回	jiàn kāng 208. 健 康
gù shi 153. 故 事	hào 171. 号	huí dá 191. 回 答	jiàn miàn 209. 见 面

210.	jiǎng 讲	230.	jīng guò 经过	248.	kě néng 可能	266.	lèi 累

jiǎng	jīng guò	kě néng	lèi
210. 讲	230. 经过	248. 可能	266. 累
jiāo	jīng lǐ	kě yǐ	lěng
211. 教	231. 经理	249. 可以	267. 冷
jiǎo	jiǔ	kè	lí
212. 角	232. 九	250. 刻	268. 离
jiǎo	jiǔ	kè	lí kāi
213. 脚	233. 久	251. 课	269. 离开
jiào	jiù	kè rén	lǐ
214. 叫	234. 旧	252. 客人	270. 里
jiào shì	jiù	kōng tiáo	lǐ wù
215. 教室	235. 就	253. 空调	271. 礼物
jiē	jǔ xíng	kǒu	lǐ shǐ
216. 接	236. 举行	254. 口	272. 历史
jiē dào	jù zi	kū	liǎn
217. 街道	237. 句子	255. 哭	273. 脸
jié hūn	jué de	kù zi	liàn xí
218. 结婚	238. 觉得	256. 裤子	274. 练习
jié shù	jué dìng	kuài	liǎng
219. 结束	239. 决定	257. 块	275. 两
jié mù		kuài	liàng
220. 节目		258. 快	276. 辆
jié rì	**K**	kuài lè	liǎo jiě
221. 节日		259. 快乐	277. 了解
jiě jie	kā fēi	kuài zi	lín jū
222. 姐姐	240. 咖啡	260. 筷子	278. 邻居
jiě jué	kāi		líng
223. 解决	241. 开		279. 零
jiè	kāi shǐ	**L**	liù
224. 借	242. 开始		280. 六
jiè shào	kàn	lái	lóu
225. 介绍	243. 看	261. 来	281. 楼
jīn tiān	kàn jiàn	lán	lù
226. 今天	244. 看见	262. 蓝	282. 路
jìn	kǎo shì	lǎo	lǚ yóu
227. 进	245. 考试	263. 老	283. 旅游
jìn	kě	lǎo shī	lù
228. 近	246. 渴	264. 老师	284. 绿
jīng cháng	kě ài	le	
229. 经常	247. 可爱	265. 了	

M

285. 妈妈 mā ma

286. 马 mǎ

287. 马 上 mǎ shàng

288. 吗 ma

289. 买 mǎi

290. 卖 mài

291. 满 意 mǎn yì

292. 慢 màn

293. 忙 máng

294. 猫 māo

295. 帽 子 mào zi

296. 没 méi

297. 没 关 系 méi guān xì

298. 每 měi

299. 妹 妹 mèi mei

300. 门 mén

301. 米 mǐ

302. 米 饭 mǐ fàn

303. 面 包 miàn bāo

304. 面 条 miàn tiáo

305. 明 白 míng bai

306. 明 天 míng tiān

307. 名 字 míng zi

N

308. 拿 ná

309. 哪(哪 儿) nǎ nǎr

310. 那（那 儿) nà nàr

311. 奶 奶 nǎi nai

312. 南 nán

313. 男 人 nán rén

314. 难 nán

315. 难 过 nán guò

316. 呢 ne

317. 能 néng

318. 你 nǐ

319. 年 nián

320. 年 级 nián jí

321. 年 轻 nián qīng

322. 鸟 niǎo

323. 您 nín

324. 牛 奶 niú nǎi

325. 努 力 nǔ lì

326. 女 儿 nǚ ér

327. 女 人 nǚ rén

P

328. 爬 山 pá shān

329. 盘 子 pán zi

330. 旁 边 páng biān

331. 胖 pàng

332. 跑 步 pǎo bù

333. 朋 友 péng you

334. 啤 酒 pí jiǔ

335. 便 宜 pián yi

336. 票 piào

337. 漂 亮 piào liang

338. 苹 果 píng guǒ

339. 葡 萄 pú táo

340. 普 通 话 pǔ tōng huà

Q

341. 七 qī

342. 妻 子 qī zi

343. 其 实 qí shí

344. 其 他 qí tā

345. 骑 qí

346. 奇 怪 qí guài

347. 起 床 qǐ chuáng

348. 千 qiān

349. 铅 笔 qiān bǐ

350. 钱 qián

351. 前 面 qián miàn

352. 清 楚 qīng chu

353. 晴 qíng

354. 请 qǐng

355. 秋 qiū

356. 去 qù

qù nián 357. 去年	shàng 373. 上	shǒu jī 393. 手机	**T**
qún zi 358. 裙子	shàng bān 374. 上班	shòu 394. 瘦	
	shàng wǎng 375. 上网	shū 395. 书	tā 413. 他
R	shàng wǔ 376. 上午	shū fu 396. 舒服	tā 414. 她
rán hòu 359. 然后	shǎo 377. 少	shū shu 397. 叔叔	tā 415. 它
ràng 360. 让	shéi 378. 谁	shù 398. 树	tài 416. 太
rè 361. 热	shēn tǐ 379. 身体	shù xué 399. 数学	tài yáng 417. 太阳
rè qíng 362. 热情	shén me 380. 什么	shuā yá 400. 刷牙	táng 418. 糖
rén 363. 人	shēng bìng 381. 生病	shuāng 401. 双	tè bié 419. 特别
rèn shi 364. 认识	shēng qì 382. 生气	shuǐ 402. 水	téng 420. 疼
rèn wéi 365. 认为	shēng rì 383. 生日	shuǐ guǒ 403. 水果	tī zú qiú 421. 踢足球
rèn zhēn 366. 认真	shēng yīn 384. 声音	shuǐ píng 404. 水平	tí 422. 题
rì 367. 日	shí 385. 十	shuì jiào 405. 睡觉	tí gāo 423. 提高
róng yì 368. 容易	shí hou 386. 时候	shuō huà 406. 说话	tǐ yù 424. 体育
rú guǒ 369. 如果	shí jiān 387. 时间	sī jī 407. 司机	tiān qì 425. 天气
	shǐ 388. 使	sì 408. 四	tián 426. 甜
	shì 389. 是	sòng 409. 送	tiáo 427. 条
S	shì jiè 390. 世界	suī rán 410. 虽然	tiào wǔ 428. 跳舞
sān 370. 三	shì qing 391. 事情	suì 411. 岁	tīng 429. 听
sǎn 371. 伞	shǒu biǎo 392. 手表	suǒ yǐ 412. 所以	tóng shì 430. 同事
shāng diàn 372. 商店			

431. 同学 tóng xué

432. 同意 tóng yì

433. 头发 tóu fa

434. 突然 tū rán

435. 图书馆 tú shū guǎn

436. 腿 tuǐ

W

437. 外 wài

438. 完 wán

439. 完成 wán chéng

440. 玩 wán

441. 碗 wǎn

442. 晚上 wǎn shang

443. 万 wàn

444. 忘记 wàng jì

445. 喂 wèi

446. 为 wèi

447. 为了 wèi le

448. 为什么 wèi shén me

449. 位 wèi

450. 文化 wén huà

451. 问 wèn

452. 问题 wèn tí

453. 我 wǒ

454. 我们 wǒ men

455. 五 wǔ

X

456. 西 xī

457. 西瓜 xī guā

458. 希望 xī wàng

459. 习惯 xí guàn

460. 洗 xǐ

461. 洗手间 xǐ shǒu jiān

462. 洗澡 xǐ zǎo

463. 喜欢 xǐ huan

464. 下 xià

465. 下午 xià wǔ

466. 下雨 xià yǔ

467. 夏 xià

468. 先 xiān

469. 先生 xiān sheng

470. 现在 xiàn zài

471. 香蕉 xiāng jiāo

472. 相同 xiāng tóng

473. 相信 xiāng xìn

474. 想 xiǎng

475. 向 xiàng

476. 像 xiàng

477. 小 xiǎo

478. 小姐 xiǎo jiě

479. 小时 xiǎo shí

480. 小心 xiǎo xīn

481. 笑 xiào

482. 校长 xiào zhǎng

483. 些 xiē

484. 鞋 xié

485. 写 xiě

486. 谢谢 xiè xie

487. 新 xīn

488. 新闻 xīn wén

489. 新鲜 xīn xiān

490. 信 xìn

491. 星期 xīng qī

492. 行李箱 xíng li xiāng

493. 姓 xìng

494. 兴趣 xìng qù

495. 熊猫 xióng māo

496. 休息 xiū xi

497. 需要 xū yào

498. 选择 xuǎn zé

499. 学生 xué sheng

500. 学习 xué xí

501. 学校 xué xiào

502. 雪 xuě

Y

503. 颜色 yán sè

504. 眼镜 yǎn jìng

yǎn jing
505. 眼 睛

yáng ròu
506. 羊 肉

yāo qiú
507. 要 求

yào
508. 药

yào
509. 要

yé ye
510. 爷 爷

yě
511. 也

yī
512. 一

yī fu
513. 衣 服

yī shēng
514. 医 生

yī yuàn
515. 医 院

yí dìng
516. 一 定

yí gòng
517. 一 共

yíhuìr
518. 一 会 儿

yí yàng
519. 一 样

yǐ hòu
520. 以 后

yǐ qián
521. 以 前

yǐ wéi
522. 以 为

yǐ jīng
523. 已 经

yǐ zi
524. 椅 子

yì bān
525. 一 般

yì biān
526. 一 边

yì qǐ
527. 一 起

yì zhí
528. 一 直

yì si
529. 意 思

yīn
530. 阴

yīn wèi
531. 因 为

yīn yuè
532. 音 乐

yín háng
533. 银 行

yīng gāi
534. 应 该

yǐng xiǎng
535. 影 响

yòng
536. 用

yóu xì
537. 游 戏

yóu yǒng
538. 游 泳

yǒu
539. 有

yǒu míng
540. 有 名

yòu
541. 又

yòu bian
542. 右 边

yú
543. 鱼

yù dào
544. 遇 到

yuán
545. 元

yuǎn
546. 远

yuàn yì
547. 愿 意

yuè
548. 月

yuè liang
549. 月 亮

yuè
550. 越

yún
551. 云

yùn dòng
552. 运 动

Z

zài
553. 在

zài
554. 再

zài jiàn
555. 再 见

zǎo shang
556. 早 上

zěn me
557. 怎 么

zěn me yàng
558. 怎 么 样

zhàn
559. 站

zhāng
560. 张

zhǎng
561. 长

zhàng fu
562. 丈 夫

zháo jí
563. 着 急

zhǎo
564. 找

zhào gù
565. 照 顾

zhào piàn
566. 照 片

zhào xiàng jī
567. 照 相 机

zhè zhèr
568. 这（这儿）

zhe
569. 着

zhēn
570. 真

zhèng zài
571. 正 在

zhī dào
572. 知 道

zhǐ
573. 只

Zhōng guó
574. 中 国

zhōng jiān
575. 中 间

zhōng wǔ
576. 中 午

zhōng yú
577. 终 于

zhǒng
578. 种

zhòng yào
579. 重 要

zhōu mò
580. 周 末

zhǔ yào
581. 主 要

zhù
582. 住

zhù	zì diǎn	zuì	zuò
583. 祝	588. 字典	593. 最	598. 做
zhù yì	zì jǐ	zuì jìn	zuò yè
584. 注意	589. 自己	594. 最近	599. 作业
zhǔn bèi	zì xíng chē	zuó tiān	zuò yòng
585. 准备	590. 自行车	595. 昨天	600. 作用
zhuō zi	zǒng shì	zuǒ bian	
586. 桌子	591. 总是	596. 左边	
zì	zǒu	zuò	
587. 字	592. 走	597. 坐	